From Portraits to Selfies

Contents

1 Hello!	2
2 The very first portraits	6
3 Formal portraits	8
4 Self-portraits	24
5 Portraits in photography	30
6 The stories in portraits	34
7 Portraits today	46
Glossary	52
Index	53
Creating a portrait	54

Written by Joe Haddow

with Royal Museums Greenwich

Collins

1 Hello!

Hello there! I'm Joe. I'm the author of this book, which I've put together with the help of some brilliant, art-loving people at Royal Museums Greenwich.

This book is about PORTRAITS!

I have a question for you. Have you ever taken a selfie?

I thought so.

Here's another one. *WHY* do we take selfies?

Hmmmm – now that's a bit tougher, isn't it?

There's probably no right or wrong answer, to be honest.

In this book, we're going to look at how the selfie came about, through the history of portraiture and the invention of the camera.

When you're at home, look around you. How many images of you and your family and friends can you see?

Have a go!

Think about a photo you've been in recently. Consider when it was taken, and why. Who took it? Does it **evoke** a fun memory? What else can you see in the picture, other than the people?

The idea of having images of you and your family and friends on walls dates back many years.

For centuries, many people have wanted lifelike images of themselves on display. Essentially, "the selfie" was created when people started paying artists to capture lifelike images of themselves.

More on that later …

To get started, let's find out what we mean when we use the word "portrait".

A portrait can be a painting, a drawing, a photograph or even a sculpture which captures people at a particular time and place. We can often find portraits in museums and art galleries, as well as our own homes!

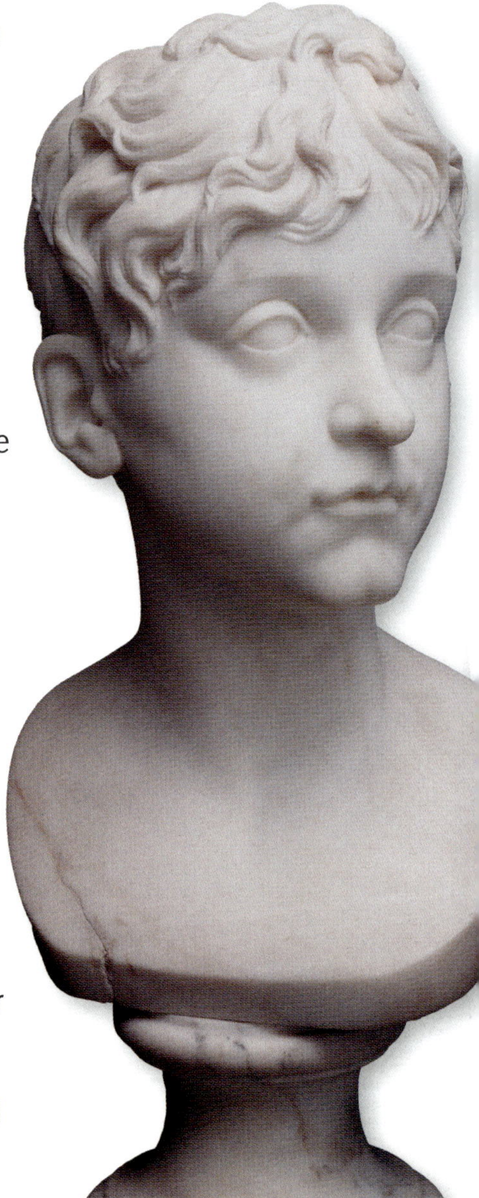

Horatia Nelson, by Christopher Prosperi (1811)

Anne of Denmark, by John de Critz (about 1605)

Reynante Concordia, At Sea, by Paul Duke (2012)

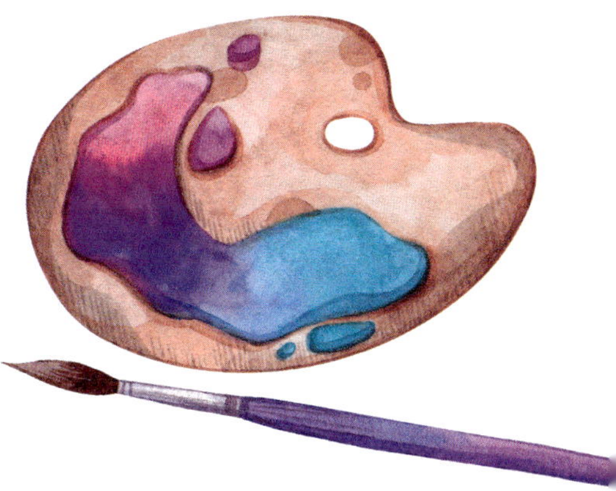

2 The very first portraits

Portraiture is a very old art form. It's SO old that the first portrait is attributed to the Egyptian empire. This means that portraiture has existed for about 5,000 years!

The ancient Egyptians gathered minerals from the earth, then crushed and mixed them with a binder to make a paint. They drew pictures to record their lives.

wall paintings from the tomb of Tutankhamun, Egypt (1327 BCE)

They often painted people from a sideways perspective, rather than head-on. This is because ancient artists couldn't make a person look realistic from a frontal perspective. The concept of drawing people from all sides hadn't been invented then.

3 Formal portraits

Let's look at the sort of people who are featured in portraits.

Portraiture in England started to become very popular around 500 years ago, at the start of the Tudor reign. We're talking the 1490s and early 1500s – a LONG time ago!

In about 1505 King Henry VII decided he wanted a lifelike painting of himself, because … you know … he was the king and what he wanted, he got. He also considered himself important enough to have a portrait.

But the reason Henry VII's portrait is such an important one is because he wanted the painter to capture his likeness. Previously, monarchs had been depicted in a symbolic, romanticised way. By this I mean the artist would flatter the sitter, making them look better than they did in real life, emphasising certain qualities and making an idealised version of the person for the world to see.

Henry VII's portrait, however, looks very realistic.

King Henry VII, by an unknown English artist (about 1505)

It was painted to show Maximilian I (the Holy Roman Emperor) what Henry looked like. Maximilian was looking for a suitable husband for his daughter Margaret, so the portrait was made to show the true likeness of Henry, not to flatter him!

It was during Henry's reign that portraiture started to become more popular across the world.

Do you know Henry VIII? (I don't mean personally.)

Well, he followed in his father's footsteps when he became king in 1509, and brought painters from all over the world to create portraits of him and his wives (he had six wives).

Here's a very famous portrait of Henry VIII.

I think it's quite striking that King Henry completely fills the canvas. It makes me think of how powerful he thought he was and his sense of self-importance.

The painting is also instantly recognisable as Henry VIII – this is how we imagine him looking. I've spoken about "the sitter", meaning the person who is posing for a portrait, but often portraitists didn't paint with the person in front of them – they based their artworks on images made by other artists.

The gold, brown and red colours in his robe make him look powerful and important.

King Henry VIII, by the studio of Hans Holbein (1500s)

That means that over the years, a lot of portraits have **perpetuated** specific images of certain people and their likeness. A lot of portraits of Henry VIII look very similar to each other because all paintings of him were influenced by the one that went before.

Traditionally, portraits were just for the monarchy or **aristocracy** who were the only people who could afford to pay for them.

King Henry VIII, by Hans Holbein the Younger (about 1640)

King Henry VIII, by Hans Eworth (about 1560)

Here's another impressive portrait of a monarch! This is Queen Elizabeth I wearing a pearl-encrusted dress, with her hand resting on a globe, implying her power and status around the world. The identity of the artist is unknown, but we *do* know that the painting was made to **commemorate** the defeat of the **Spanish Armada** in 1588.

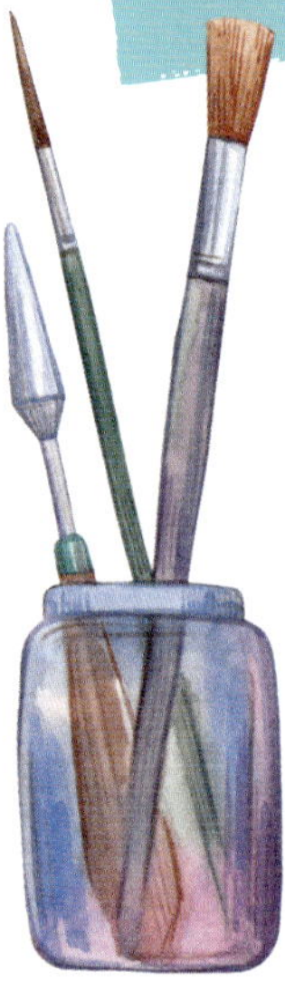

You can see the Armada being wrecked in a storm behind her!

The Armada Portrait of Queen Elizabeth I, by an unknown English artist (about 1588)

The Armada Portrait is a very big painting, which enhances its feeling of power, but portraits can come in all shapes and sizes. Take this one, for example …

This is a portrait of Indian political leader Zeenat Mahal, which was painted around 1840. It's a portable portrait, meaning it could fit in a pocket (like a photo on a smartphone) and be carried around.

Miniatures were often given as gifts, so this piece could have been for an important member of Zeenat's family, and was maybe even part of a piece of jewellery, so the owner could wear it.

actual size!

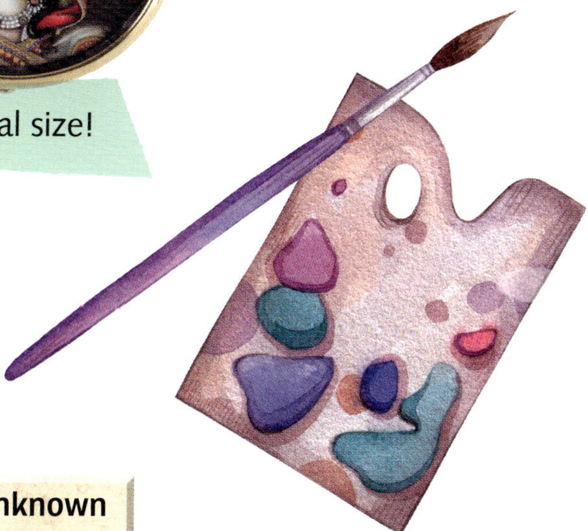

Zeenat Mahal, by an unknown Indian artist (about 1840)

Not all portraits are painted, though. A portrait can be made as a sculpture.

Take this one, for example …

This is a **stylised bust** of Jean-Jacques Dessalines, carved out of wood.

Who's this, then? I hear you ask …

Well, Jean-Jacques was born into slavery in Haiti in 1758, but in 1791 became part of the freedom movement that led to the **abolition** of slavery there. In 1804, he became the first emperor of Haiti. He's regarded as the founder of independent Haiti.

Can you see that he's wearing a military-style uniform and hat? The sculpture certainly makes him look important, doesn't it? We don't know where it was made, but the style of the carving matches sculptures made in West Africa, so this sculpture may be reflecting the African **heritage** of enslaved people in Haiti.

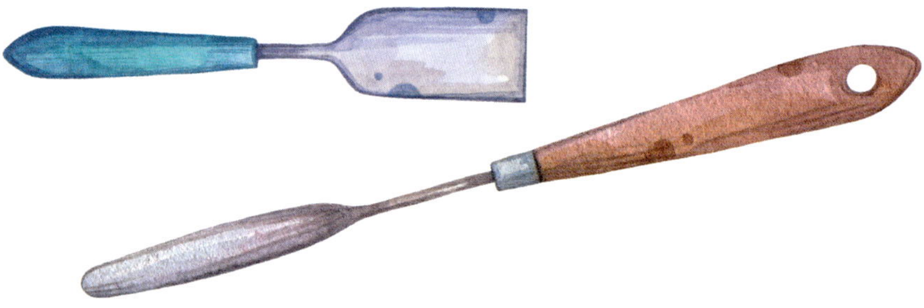

Jean-Jacques Dessalines, by an unknown artist (1800s)

Can I tell you about William Hogarth?

He was an English painter and satirist (an artist who used humour in his work to make fun of people).

Now, it's important to know that at the time Hogarth was working, in the 18th century, a wider range of people were commissioning portraits, and the style of portraiture changed. Artists started painting more informally, putting more emphasis on individuality rather than sticking to a traditional, formal style.

Here's a Hogarth painting, which he made between 1730 and 1735. It shows a family together having a tea party.

As you can see, it's an active scene and not formally posed – the characters are looking at each other rather than the viewer. There are lots of interesting details in the picture, too, that can give us some hints as to what we're looking at.

Can you see there's a servant holding out a tray to one of the family members? We can only see the person's arms and hands because this picture was cut down to be smaller at some point.

The Family of John, 2nd Duke of Montagu and an Attendant, by William Hogarth (1730–35)

Did you spot the sewing basket spilling its contents – and a guilty-looking kitten close by?

Hogarth's style was very detailed, to the point where he was criticised for his "minute exactness" by fellow painter and founder of the Royal Academy of Arts, Joshua Reynolds.

Hogarth drew people as he saw them, and that attention to detail, mixed with satire, meant his portraits didn't always flatter the subject. Because of this, they were often rejected by the sitter, for being "too real".

What people in the present day love about his paintings, though, is that they give us a view of society at the time. And his paintings show a range of people from different social classes.

So, as you can see, anyone can be the subject of a portrait, they don't have to be a king or queen!

The Strode Family, by William Hogarth, c1738.

4 Self-portraits

As well as portraits, there are also SELF portraits.

A self-portrait is exactly what you think it is – it's when an artist paints, draws, sculpts or photographs themselves – either in a very lifelike, recognisable way, or in an abstract way, depicting themselves symbolically or uncharacteristically.

It's believed the first known example of a painted self-portrait is by Dutch artist Jan van Eyck, from 1433. It's called, quite simply, *Portrait of A Man*.

(I'm not one to judge, but I probably could have come up with a slightly more exciting title than that. Couldn't you?)

His eyes are really gazing at us, aren't they? Or maybe he's staring at himself in a mirror? That's perfectly possible, as that's the way many artists make a self-portrait of themselves.

Either way, it feels very much like he's watching us, or judging us even (maybe because I made that comment about the title of his painting)!

I find it very lifelike and detailed. It's quite amazing that it was painted almost 600 years ago.

This red headdress is known as a chaperon, which was fashionable for men in the 15th century.

Portrait of a Man,
by Jan van Eyck (1433)

Let's look at another one! (I'm getting excited now.)

Here's an example of a more modern self-portrait.

This is a very well-known painting by a very famous and celebrated artist – Vincent van Gogh.

Self-Portrait with a Straw Hat, by Vincent van Gogh (1880s)

van Gogh was a Dutch painter, born in 1853. You might know some of his work, such as *"Sunflowers" or "The Starry Night".*

He made A LOT of paintings during his lifetime that have become popular. But would you believe it, he only sold one painting when he was alive!

Between 1886 and 1888, he painted 22 self-portraits when he was living with his brother in Paris, and this is one of them.

This painting has become one of the most famous self-portraits in the world. It's in van Gogh's unique style, using bright colours and short brushstrokes.

The reason I think it's so interesting and important is that he is using this image to show us his failing health. The shadows and his closed and quite tight mouth suggest someone who isn't particularly happy and may well be in pain, both physically and emotionally, which we now know poor van Gogh was.

In this self-portrait, you can make out the artist very clearly. He has painted an accurate likeness of himself, and we instantly recognise his style.

Auto-Portrait,
by Chila Kumari Burman (1996–2013)

Here's an example of a much more modern self-portrait. It's by the British artist Chila Kumari Burman. Here, she has used smaller photos to create her own larger self-portrait. It took over ten years to finish! I think it's really striking to have so many faces staring back at you – each one could represent a different life story to tell.

Have a go!

If you like the idea of making your own self-portrait, here's a little exercise for you ...

Get a piece of paper and a pencil. Sit at a table and prop up a mirror (a small one – don't go trying to take the big one off the wall!).

Set the mirror up so you can see yourself, then start to sketch out the outline of your head on the paper. Do the outer edges first, and the tops of your shoulders if you want to, then start filling in the detail (like your eyes, nose and mouth).

You might choose to draw yourself in a lifelike way or be a bit abstract – there's no right or wrong here. Create your own style!

5 Portraits in photography

Remember at the beginning of this book, I asked if you had ever taken a selfie? Well, I think it's fair to say that a selfie is actually a self-portrait.

And here's why … let me take you way back to 1839.

This is the year that Robert Cornelius (a chemist and photographer) took the very first example of self-portrait photography.

He took this photo by removing the lens cap of his camera, then moving in front of it, where he sat still for a whole minute.

This is what cameras looked like when Robert Cornelius was taking his first photo!

Self-Portrait, by Robert Cornelius (1839)

The invention of the camera was revolutionary and meant that thousands of people have been recorded in images who would otherwise have faded from history.

As the technology of cameras moved on, they became cheaper and more accessible. Events could be captured in the moment.

Now, we can instantly take a snapshot of our lives wherever we are and whenever we want, on our phones.

But while photography became incredibly popular, and still is, it never fully replaced the formal portrait.

Do you see now why I think the history of the selfie can be traced back to portraiture?

Think about any selfie you have taken, or photo that's been taken of you. The moment the lens is on you, you pose – you pull a face or move the way you're standing, to present the image you want the viewer to see.

Even animals pose. Look at this selfie, taken by a female crested black macaque monkey in Indonesia.

This was taken in 2011, when British photographer David Slater visited a national park in North Sulawesi, Indonesia.

He left his camera and found this photo on it later, showing that the monkey had been exploring his equipment and accidentally taken a photo.

Does this classify as a self-portrait, do you think? I DO!

6 The stories in portraits

So, what should we look for in a portrait? What story does the artist want to tell us?

The first thing to say is that, much like photos on social media or in the news, portraits tell a version of a story and show a person in a particular way. Sometimes it's how *they* want us to see them, sometimes it's how the *artist* wants us to see them – and often, it's a bit of both.

After all, an artist will always have their own unique style and will represent things the way they see them.

Those who are being painted may also try to hide certain things or be captured in a way that highlights what they believe are their strong attributes. Take, for example, Thomas Gainsborough's portrait of Captain Frederick Cornewall …

Here you can see that his pose highlights his missing arm. His empty sleeve is prominent at the front of the picture, for us to see. His right arm was amputated after he was wounded in battle. Frederick's wound was seen as proof that he was a "fighting officer" – and he continued to serve in the Royal Navy for another 18 years after the injury.

Captain Frederick Cornewall, by Thomas Gainsborough (1762)

Can you see – his sleeve is attached to a button on his coat to hold it up.

Cornewall commissioned his portrait in 1762, to celebrate his retirement. He chose to draw attention to his missing arm, turning that side of the body towards the viewer, which could be to prove that he had risked life and limb for his country.

What's interesting about the Cornewall portrait is that there are no ships in the background. Traditionally, naval portraits included the image of a ship or ships – like this one on the right here.

In the background of this portrait, you can see an English and a Dutch ship in combat. These are referencing Richard Deane's service in the First Anglo-Dutch War (a conflict between the English and Dutch from 1652 to 1654).

In contrast, the portrait of Captain Frederick Cornewall has a plain dark background, highlighting that he was retiring and would no longer be captain of a ship.

Richard Deane, General at Sea, by Robert Walker (about 1653)

We've looked at how people are dressed and the colours that are used to represent certain themes (power, wealth and personality, for example) but we haven't yet talked about props, which can be very important in portraiture.

Take this painting of Sir Kenelm Digby by his friend, Anthony van Dyck, for example …

"Who's this guy?" I hear you ask.

Sir Kenelm Digby, by the studio of Anthony van Dyck (1630s)

Well, he was a philosopher, astrologer, poet, and diplomat with an adventurous and inquisitive spirit. He sailed the world, commanded two ships and wrote romantic stories!

But his life was also full of tragedy. This portrait was painted quite soon after the death of his wife.

What else can you see in the picture?

A SUNFLOWER! YES. But why?

Is it a symbol of Sir Kenelm's loyalty to King Charles I, suggesting that he followed the king like the sunflower follows the sun?

Or is it a symbol of learning? Sir Kenelm was an academic, so is it a suggestion of him following the light of wisdom like the sunflower follows the sunlight?

It could refer to the nickname he was given – "Il Fiorito" – which means "the flowery one" in Italian?

Or maybe he just loved sunflowers!

It could be none of these things. The portrait is open to our interpretation, and that's important to remember when looking at any art. You'll see things differently and get a different meaning from art than another person.

You know when you take a photo and you don't like a particular part of it, so you run it through a filter to make it look better?

Well, believe it or not, artists have been doing this for centuries!

Have a look at this painting by Joshua Reynolds.

This is Captain the Honourable Augustus Keppel. (Quite a name, isn't it!)

You can see him pictured here on a stormy beach, with debris from a shipwreck in the waves. A very dramatic setting!

It shows Augustus Keppel in the aftermath of a disaster, taking charge. He clearly wanted to emphasise the danger of his work as a naval officer.

Look how the cliffs and trees loom over him, adding to the drama of the picture.

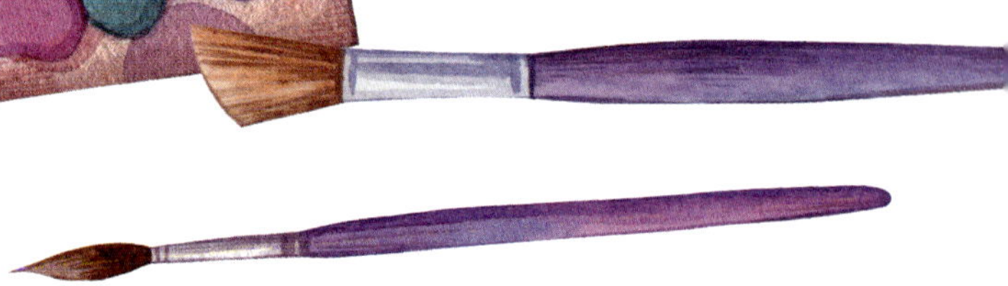

Captain the Honourable Augustus Keppel,
by Joshua Reynolds (1752–53)

Now have a look at the image on the right. This is an X-ray of the central section of the painting. Can you see any differences in the background compared with the finished painting?

So, what does this mean then, Joe?

Well, the X-ray shows that this portrait was originally painted with a very different setting. Keppel was painted in front of a building with a large column.

But this was painted over. Augustus must have changed his mind and wanted something more dramatic. So, the storm, waves and beach were all added on instead.

The idea of having a column behind him was very traditional at the time. Most portraits had a piece of architecture in the background, to create a sense of importance. By changing this to a shipwreck, though, it created a sense of action. It's like we're seeing him in the middle of a dramatic situation. This was also a way the artist, Joshua Reynolds, could show off his skills, because painting movement and action is more challenging than buildings.

You see! Artists have been putting filters on their work for years.

You can see how Reynolds has changed the position of Augustus Keppel's head.

There's a big column right here in the background that we can't see in the finished painting.

On the right is a self-portrait painted around the year 1666 by the artist and businesswoman Mary Beale, who is thought to be one of the first professional female painters in Britain.

This portrait is in a similar style and pose to other portraits of women at this time, but the painting in her hand is Mary's subtle hint at the role she had in this image – she painted it!

Have a go!

If *you* were getting a portrait done, what would you want to be holding or showing in the background? Do you have a hobby perhaps that can be represented by an object? Or a favourite item at home, like a toy or gadget? Maybe there's a big event you'd want to show, like a holiday?

Why not have a go now. Grab a sheet of paper and draw out some of the objects that you would want in *your* portrait's background.

Self-Portrait,
by Mary Beale (1666)

Look what she's holding – Mary has added an unframed painting to the image to highlight that she wasn't an artist's sitter, but the artist herself!

7 Portraits today

So … are artists still painting portraits now?

They sure are! Lots in fact, all taking a lot of time and effort to capture a person in a particular environment, with hidden meanings that would be more difficult to show in a photo.

This is King Charles III, painted by Jonathan Yeo. The canvas is more than two metres tall, which is bigger than a horse!

You can see the king in the Welsh Guards uniform, holding a sword – and with a butterfly about to land on his shoulder. Jonathan started the painting when his subject was still known as The Prince of Wales (hence the uniform), but by the time the portrait was complete, he was king.

He said he added the butterfly as a symbol of rebirth, which reflects the king's transition from prince to monarch during the painting.

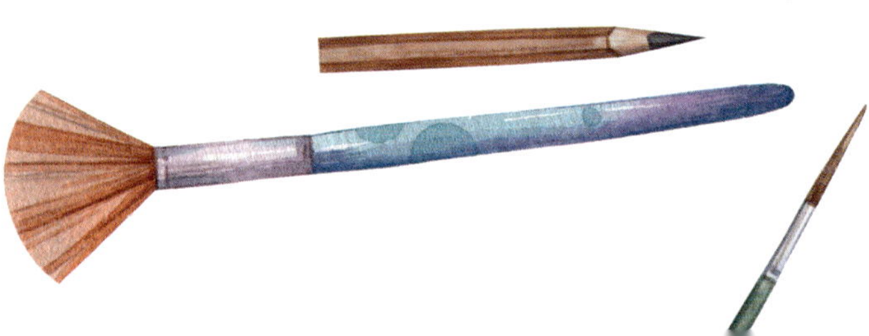

Portrait of His Majesty King Charles III, by Jonathan Yeo (2024)

Here's another brilliantly colourful portrait, from the USA.

This is a portrait of the 44th American President, Barack Obama, who made history in 2009 by becoming the first African-American president.

It's painted by the artist Kehinde Wiley, who is known for his vibrant, large-scale paintings.

Look at the flowers in the background. They all carry special meaning for Obama. The chrysanthemums, for example, reference the official flower of Chicago. The jasmine evokes Hawaii, where he spent most of his childhood, and the African blue lilies stand in for his late Kenyan father.

Once again, we're reminded that portraiture has an important place in our world, and that artists will continue to create snapshots of life, and of people, for many years.

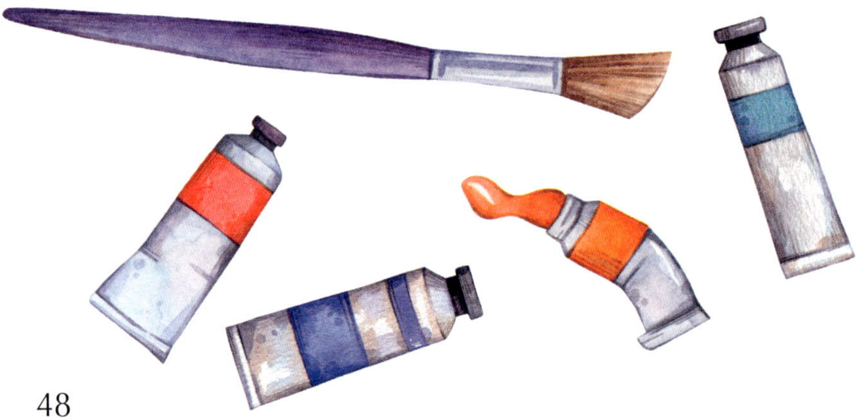

Barack Obama,
by Kehinde Wiley (2018)

Máire and Síle Scanlon, Ballycotton RNLI Lifeboat Volunteers, 14th September 2017, by Jack Lowe

WHY are portraits considered to be so important, then?

Before the invention of the camera, the *ONLY* way to record someone's existence and what they looked like (other than writing a description) was by painting, sculpting or drawing their portrait. This, for me, makes portraiture incredibly important, because it gives us a sense of time and place – and of course, a person.

Portraits are a historic record of the generations who have gone before us, and how they lived. Just being near old works of art makes me feel like I could be transported back hundreds of years.

Through the history of art, portraits were often used to represent power and status. But more recently, a portrait can come in many different forms and is often a way of exploring a person and their quirks, rather than a big status piece. I, personally, much prefer that.

So, the next time you're taking a selfie, of yourself, or with friends or family, just remember …

… you're part of an art form that's nearly 5,000 years old.

Glossary

abolition officially ending or stopping

aristocracy the highest class in societies; people are often born into it

bust a sculptural representation of the upper part of the human body

commemorate to celebrate or remember an event by doing or making something

evoke bring to mind a feeling or memory

heritage something handed down from the past, such as traditions

perpetuated something which was made to continue

Spanish Armada a fleet of powerful ships from Spain that tried to invade England in 1588

stylised something created in a non-realistic way

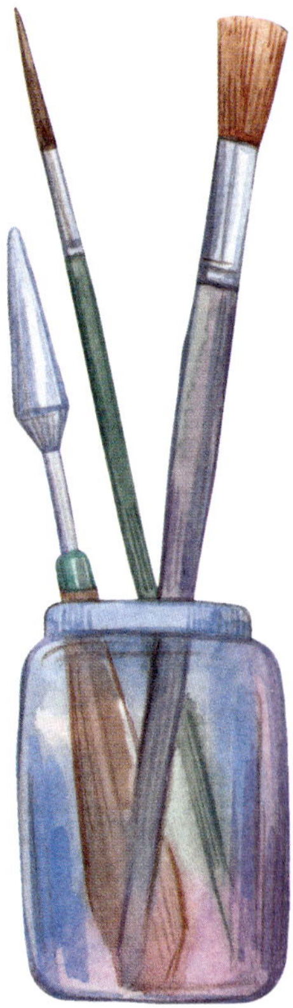

Index

ancient Egyptians 6–7

Beale, Mary 44–45

Burman, Chila Kumari 28–29

Cornelius, Robert 30–31

Dessalines, Jean-Jacques 18–19

Gainsborough, Thomas 34–35

Hogarth, William 20–23

Holbein, Hans 11–13

King Charles III 46–47

King Henry VII 8–9

King Henry VIII 10–13

Lowe, Jack 50

Mahal, Zeenat 16–17

miniatures 17

monkey 33

Obama, Barack 48–49

photography 30–33

Queen Elizabeth I 14–15

Reynolds, Joshua 40–43

sculpture 4, 18–19

selfie 2–4, 30–31, 33, 51

self-portrait 24–29, 30–31, 33, 44–45

van Dyck, Anthony 38–39

van Eyck, Jan 24–25

van Gogh, Vincent 26–27

Walker, Robert 36–37

Wiley, Kehinde 48–49

X-ray 42–43

Yeo, Jonathan 46–47

Creating a portrait

What type?

- large format

- miniature

- sculpture

- photo

What style?

- realistic

- abstract

What subject?

- portrait

- self-portrait

What stories can it tell?

- major events
- status
- job
- family
- health

Ideas for reading

Written by Gill Matthews
Primary Literacy Consultant

Reading objectives:
- check that the book makes sense to them, discuss their understanding and explore the meaning of words in context
- summarise the main ideas drawn from more than one paragraph, identifying key details that support the main ideas
- retrieve, record and present information from non-fiction

Spoken language objectives:
- use relevant strategies to build their vocabulary
- articulate and justify answers, arguments and opinions
- participate in discussions, presentations, performances, role play, improvisations and debates

Curriculum links: Art

Interest words: portraits, portraiture, lifelike, perspective, abstract

Resources: mirrors, art materials

Build a context for reading

- Ask children to look closely at the front cover and to read the title. Discuss what they think the title means.
- Read the back-cover blurb. Ask what the children expect to read about in the book.
- Point out that this is an information book. Ask what features the children expect to find in the book.
- Ask them to find the contents page. Discuss the purpose and organisation of a contents list.
- Ask the children to use the contents to find the chapter called *Hello!*

Understand and apply reading strategies

- Read pp2–5 aloud. Ask children to carry out the activity in the Have a go! box on p3. Take feedback.
- Ask questions about this chapter that involve the children scanning the text to find the answers e.g. What is the name of the author? Can you name some different types of portrait? Discuss the techniques that they used to find the answers.